Researching the impact of the National Singing Programme *'Sing Up'* in England: Main findings from the first three years (2007-2010). Children's singing development, self-concept and sense of social inclusion.

Researching the impact of the National Singing Programme 'Sing Up' in England: Main Findings from the first three years. Children's singing development, self-concept and sense of social inclusion.

Core Research Team:
Graham F. Welch
Evangelos Himonides
Jo Saunders
Ioulia Papageorgi

Additional Research Team Members:
Costanza Preti
Tiija Rinta
Maria Vraka
Cynthia Stephens Himonides
ClaireStewart
Jennifer Lanipekun
Joy Hill

ISBN13: 978-1-905351-13-8
ISBN10: 1-905351-13-5

Copyright ©2010 Graham Welch & Evangelos Himonides

Published in Great Britain in 2010
International Music Education Research Centre
http://www.imerc.org
Department of Arts and Humanities
Institute of Education
University of London
20, Bedford Way
London WC1H 0AL
United Kingdom

Copy requests:
Dr Evangelos Himonides
e.himonides@ioe.ac.uk

Typeset using LaTeX in 'Computer Modern Roman' by:
Dr Evangelos Himonides, e.himonides@ioe.ac.uk

British Library Cataloguing-in-Publication Data
A CIP record is available from the British Library

All rights reserved. Except for the quotation of short passages for the purposes of criticism or review, no part of this publication may be reproduced, stored in a retrieval system, or transmitted, in any form or by any means, electronic, mechanical, photocopying, recording or otherwise, without prior permission of the publisher.

Contents

1 **Background and Aims**   7

2 **Method**   9

3 **Main Findings**   11
    3.1 Comfortable singing range and age 11
    3.2 Comfortable singing range by school type 11
    3.3 Singing development and ethnicity 13
    3.4 Singing development and sex 13
    3.5 Singing development and school type 15
    3.6 Children's singing development and age: impact of *Sing Up* 18
    3.7 Longitudinal evidence of *Sing Up*'s impact 20
    3.8 Singing assessment and school type rankings 21
    3.9 Attitudinal evidence and *Sing Up* impact 22
    3.10 Singing development, self concept and social inclusion . 22

4 **Conclusions**   25

5 **References**   27

6 **Selected Public Output related to *Sing Up***   29

7 **Articles in refereed international journals**   31

8 **Conference Proceedings**   33

9 **Published reports**   35

10 **Other output in professional journals**   37

List of Figures

1	Number of assessments by school category and year of data collection	10
2	Comfortable mean singing range and age	12
3	Comfortable mean singing range by school type	13
4	Mean comfortable range in semitones for Singing Playgrounds children across three years (2007-2010)	14
5	Normalised singing ratings and ethnicity	14
6	Singing rating by children's sex and the number of different *Sing Up* inputs that they have experienced (one or more)	15
7	School types and normalised singing ratings by sex of participants	16
8	Mean singing development and school type	17
9	Mean singing development scores for Singing Playgrounds children by year of data collection.	17
10	Singing development and chronological age	18
11	Singing development and chronological age by school type	19
12	Longitudinal data and school type across three years	20
13	Longitudinal data and school type across two consecutive years (NSS = Normalised Singing Score — out of 100)	21
14	Self-concept and social inclusion means by quartile and normalised singing score for the same children (n=6639 children, 2008-2010)	23

List of Tables

1	Statistically similar grouping (singing development and school type)	16
2	Proportions of *Sing Up* and non-*Sing Up* schools in an overall schools' ranking by upper and lower quartiles	21

1 Background and Aims

This report provides a summative analysis of longitudinal and comparative research data from the first three years of an ongoing four-year national study of children's singing development in England (2007-2011). In the Autumn of 2007, the UK Government initiated a National Singing Programme *Sing Up* with the intention of fostering positive singing experiences each week for all children of Primary school age in England by 2011. As part of the evaluation of this programme, a research team from the Institute of Education, University of London were appointed in 2007 to conduct an independent evaluation of the programme's impact.

Key research foci have included a comparative mapping of the following:

- Children's singing behaviour and development, noting whether or not participants have had experience of the national programme; and

- Children's attitudes towards singing at school, home and elsewhere.

An additional focus since 2008 has been on:

- The possible wider impact of singing on children's self concept and sense of social inclusion.

2 Method

Children (n=9,979 to date), of whom 95% were aged 7+ to 11+ years, were drawn from 177 schools located across England in the opening three years of research, 2007-2010. The choice of schools was on the basis of an initial contact through local authority or higher education networks, with the main criterion being to ensure a diverse range of geographical and singing experienced settings, as well as social and ethnic diversity. Subsequently, additional schools were nominated to be included as examples of the different types of experiences available under the *Sing Up* programme umbrella. These included schools participating in the *Chorister Outreach Programme* (COP), *Workforce Development, Singing Playgrounds* and *Sing Up Awards* initiatives.

The first year's research (2007-2008) was designed to establish an initial 'baseline' of singing in English Primary schools against which subsequent *Sing Up* programme impact data could be compared. This first year also included data generated in relation to one particular *Sing Up* intervention, i.e., focused on children who had experienced Ex Cathedra's *'Singing Playgrounds'* initiative[1]. The second year (2008-2009) extended the number of schools and *Sing Up* intervention-related data. It also included a longitudinal component that involved re-assessing children from the first year after approximately a twelve-month interval. The third year's data collection (2009-2010) followed the same principles and included both comparative and longitudinal aspects.

Across the three years of impact data collection, children's individual singing behaviour and development were assessed by noting each individual child's performance of two well-known songs within a specially designed protocol that combined two established rating scales (Rutkowski, 1997; Welch, 1998; see Welch *et al*, 2009 for more detail, including how the singing scores were normalised). In addition, attitudes to singing, self-concept and social inclusion were assessed by a specially designed questionnaire embracing six themes[2]. In the second year, socio-economic background was assessed in relation to the UK Government's *Index of Multiple Deprivation*.

Some children were seen more than once during this period in or-

---

[1] http://www.excathedra.co.uk/singing_playgrounds.php?submenuheader=3

[2] There were five themes in the first year's questionnaire, each music related, to which a sixth theme, *self-concept and sense of social inclusion*, was included from 'year two' onwards.

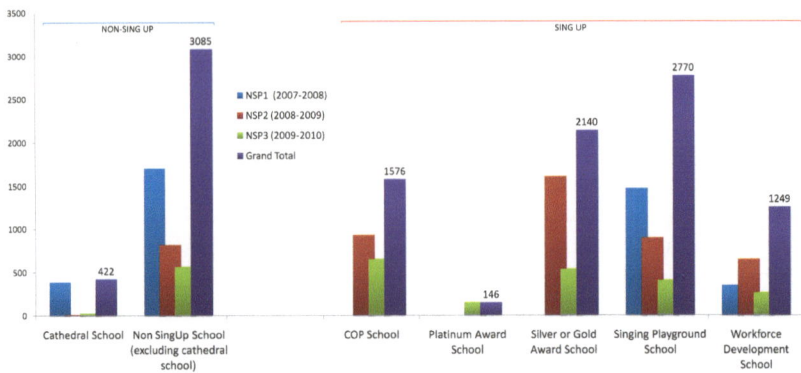

Figure 1: Number of assessments by school category and year of data collection

der to include a longitudinal perspective. Consequently, overall, the 9,979 children generated 11,388 individual singing assessments and completed 10,245 individual attitudinal questionnaires. Approximately one in three (30.8%, n=3507) were assessments of children who were outside the *Sing Up* programme at the time of their assessment. The breakdown of assessments by school category and year of data collection is shown in figure 1.

There were approximately equal numbers of girls (51.8%) and boys (48.2%). Three-quarters (75.9%) of the children were classified as 'white' according to the schools' official ethnicity data that had been gathered for official reporting to the Ministry (*DfES/DCSF* (then), *DfE* (now)), with Asian (12.4%) and Black (6.2%) being the two main ethnic minority groups. These proportions in the impact evaluation data set are similar to those in the official school statistics for England (*DCSF*, 2008)[3].

---

[3]See http://tinyurl.com/5hlvs4, retrieved 4 September 2009

3 Main Findings

There were significant age, sex, ethnicity and school type differences in the emergent findings. Within these group variables, older children, girls and national singing programme (*Sing Up*) experienced participants tended to have more advanced singing development. Of the three main ethnic groups represented, both white and black children were likely to be more highly rated in their singing competency than their Asian peers. Nevertheless, all three ethnic groups, including Asian children, were significantly more advanced in their singing development after *Sing Up* participation. Furthermore, the Year 2 data analyses had already demonstrated that there was no evidence that more competent singers came from socially advantageous settings. Age and longitudinal data indicated that children's singing competency tended to improve with age and experience, but particularly so in a stimulating musical environment, such as provided by the *Sing Up* programme. In addition, there was a strong positive correlation between children's singing development and their self-concept and sense of social inclusion.

Example details of the main findings are set out in the sections that follow.

3.1 Comfortable singing range and age

Children's mean comfortable singing range (assessed by asking children to work outwards — ascending and descending — from their speaking pitch centre using simple pitch glides) extended significantly ($p<.001$) from approximately one and half to almost two octaves in pitch from the ages of 7+y to 10+y (i.e., from an average pitch range of g_3-c_5 to f_3-$e_5^\flat$; see darkened shading in figure 2). There was no significant difference in comfortable pitch range between the two oldest age groups (ages 9+ and 10+). However, sex differences were evidenced for all age groups ($p<.001$), with girls having a wider range than boys.

3.2 Comfortable singing range by school type

An analysis was undertaken of mean comfortable singing range according to the different categories of schools in the database. This analysis

3.2 Comfortable singing range by school type

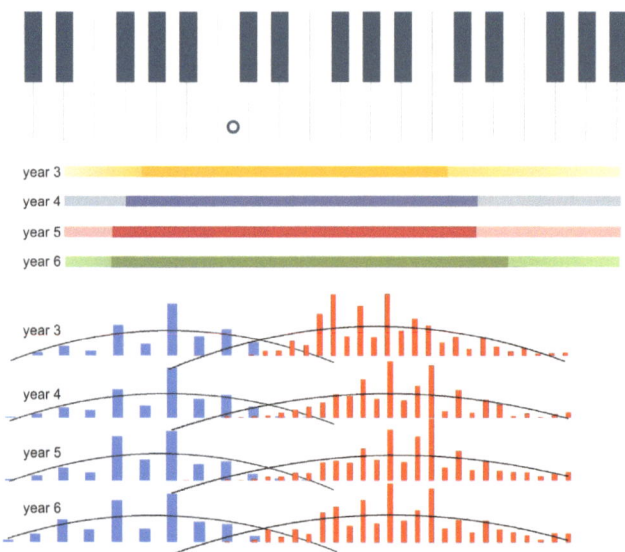

Figure 2: Comfortable mean singing range and age

indicated a general trend of increasing vocal pitch range with experience ($p<.0001$). Children who had experienced an extended programme of singing development (such as likely to be found in *Platinum Award* and *Chorister Outreach Programme* schools) tended to have the widest mean comfortable singing range as measured in semitones (see figure 3). Although there was a significant difference overall across school types, there was no difference between children from *Platinum Award schools* and *Cathedral schools* (including cathedral choristers).

The relatively limited mean comfortable singing range exhibited by children in our *Singing Playground* schools' data (compared to the other categories of schools) derives from an unintended bias in data collection. In the first year of our research (termed *NSP Year 1* in figure 4 below), singing data were collected mainly from children in school Year 3 (aged 7+) and Year 6 (aged 10+). This first year's data accounts for 53% of the overall *Singing Playgrounds* dataset and the mean comfortable singing range is 11.2 semitones. The National Singing Programme *Sing Up* had only been launched a few months earlier and had had limited opportunity for sustained impact at the time of our data collection.

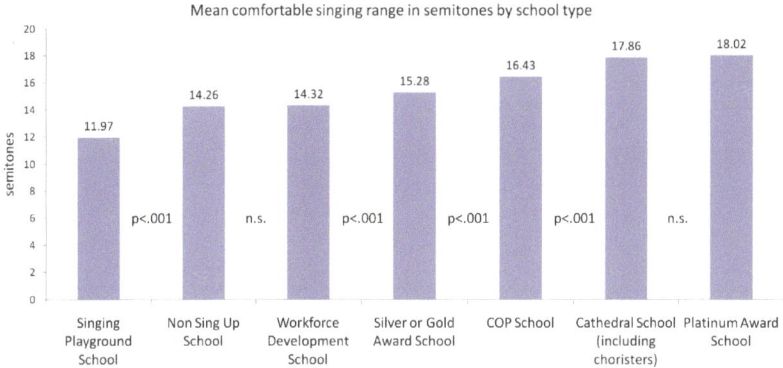

Figure 3: Comfortable mean singing range by school type

In the following year (labelled *NSP Year 2* in figure 4), the research focus shifted to children's singing in school Years 4 and 5 (ages 8+ to 9+) and there is an increase in the mean comfortable singing range to 12.1 semitones. In this past year (labelled *NSP Year 3* in figure 4), the research focus is more balanced across Key Stage 2 (ages 7+ to 10+) and the mean comfortable singing range demonstrated a further significant increase to 14.16 semitones. We suggest that this third year's dataset is probably more representative of children with experience of *Singing Playgrounds* activity than the overall average of 11.97 semitones (as displayed in figures 3 and 4).

3.3 Singing development and ethnicity

Asian children tended to have less developed singing behaviours compared to the other two major ethnic groupings represented in the data (Black and White) ($p<.001$). However, all three ethnic groupings were rated significantly higher in *Sing Up* schools (i.e., schools that had participated in the *Sing Up* programme) (see figure 5).

3.4 Singing development and sex

In general, girls tended to be rated as significantly more developed in their singing compared to boys ($p<.0001$). Somewhat surprisingly, this

3.4 Singing development and sex

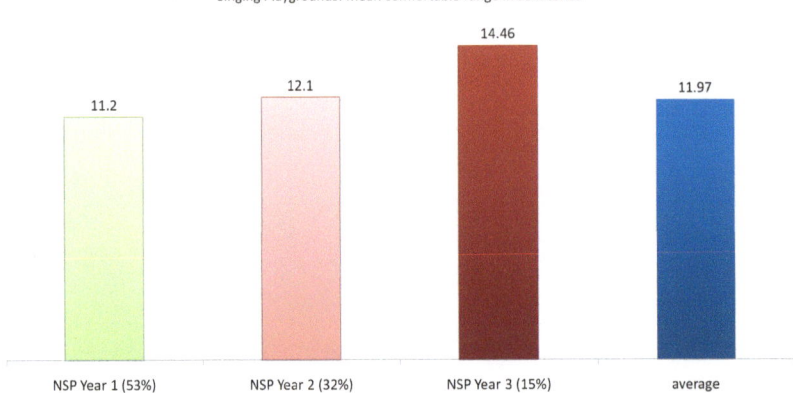

Figure 4: Mean comfortable range in semitones for Singing Playgrounds children across three years (2007-2010)
Note: The figures in parentheses represent the relative size of this yearly cohort within the overall Singing Playgrounds dataset.

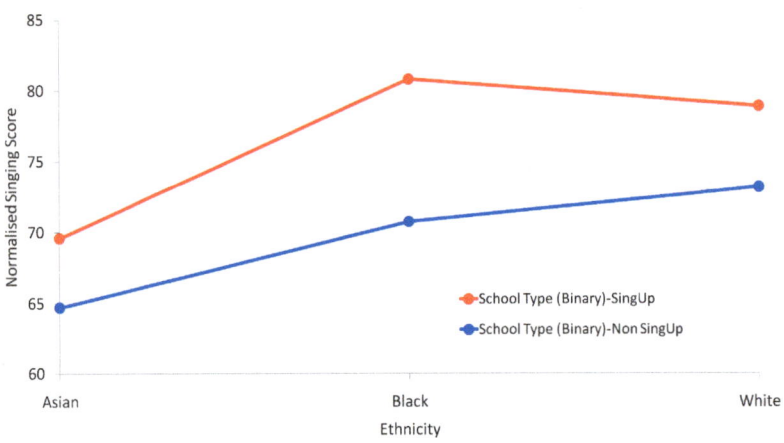

Figure 5: Normalised singing ratings and ethnicity

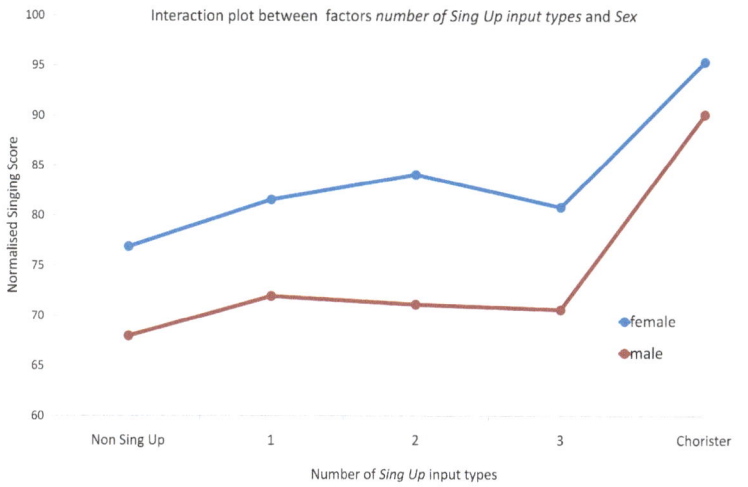

Figure 6: Singing rating by children's sex and the number of different *Sing Up* inputs that they have experienced (one or more)

sex difference persists despite the number of different *Sing Up* interventions experienced by the children (see figure 6), although we recognise that increasing the number of *Sing Up* experiences (such as using the *Song Bank*, being in an *Award school*) does not necessarily imply a multiplying effect. However, the singing development ratings of male and female choristers were statistically similar.

Nevertheless, although this sex difference also persists across school types (figure 7), it is differentially evidenced in the longitudinal data (see figures 9 and 10).

3.5 Singing development and school type

Nevertheless, children from schools that had experience of *Sing Up* tended to have higher singing development ratings than their non-*Sing Up* peers (see figure 8). Although the cathedral choristers — perhaps not unsurprisingly — achieved the highest ratings, these ratings are statistically similar to those from children who had participated in the *Chorister Outreach Programme*. (*Note:* Table 1, included underneath the figure, demonstrates statistical similarities in the clustering of mean

3.5 Singing development and school type

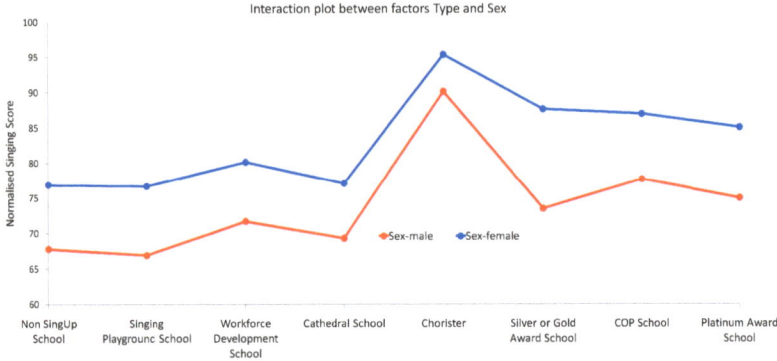

Figure 7: School types and normalised singing ratings by sex of participants

Categories	Mean	Groupings			
Chorister	90.925	A			
COP School	83.549	A			
Silver or Gold Award School	80.579		B		
Platinum Award School	79.598		B	C	
Workforce Development School	75.770			C	
Cathedral School	72.440				D
Non Sing Up School	72.376				D
Singing Playground School	71.898				D

Table 1: Statistically similar grouping (singing development and school type)

ratings by school type.)

As mentioned earlier in the discussion on mean comfortable singing range, the *Singing Playground* data is biased towards the first year of the data collection (for example, as illustrated in figure 1), that is, early in the *Sing Up* programme, which explains why these children's mean ratings overall are similar to those in non-*Sing Up* school types (including non-choristers in cathedral schools). When the composite singing data is broken by year of collection (figure 9), it is clear that there is an upward trend, with children in the third year (2009-2010) having their singing assessed at the same mean level of development as children in *Award schools*.

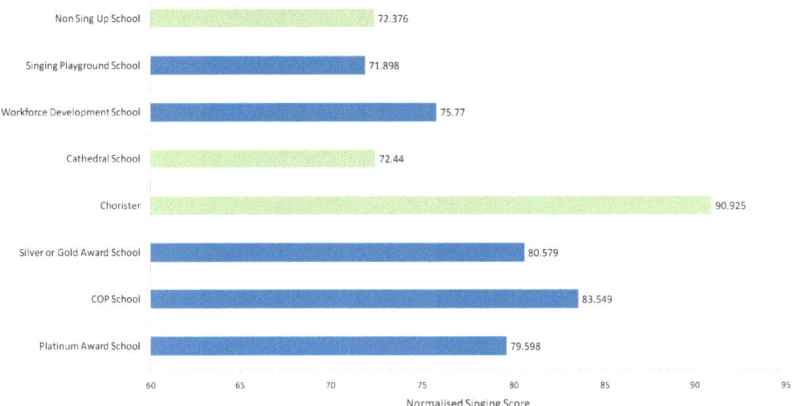

Figure 8: Mean singing development and school type

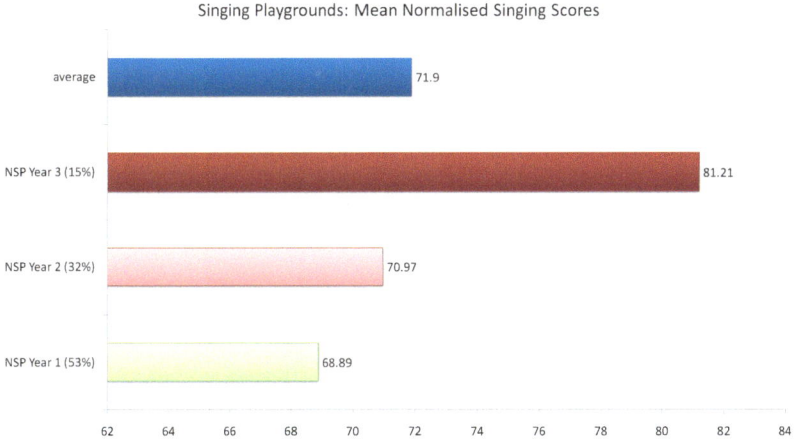

Figure 9: Mean singing development scores for Singing Playgrounds children by year of data collection.
Note: The figures in parentheses represent the relative size of this yearly cohort within the overall Singing Playgrounds dataset.

3.6 Children's singing development and age: impact of *Sing Up*

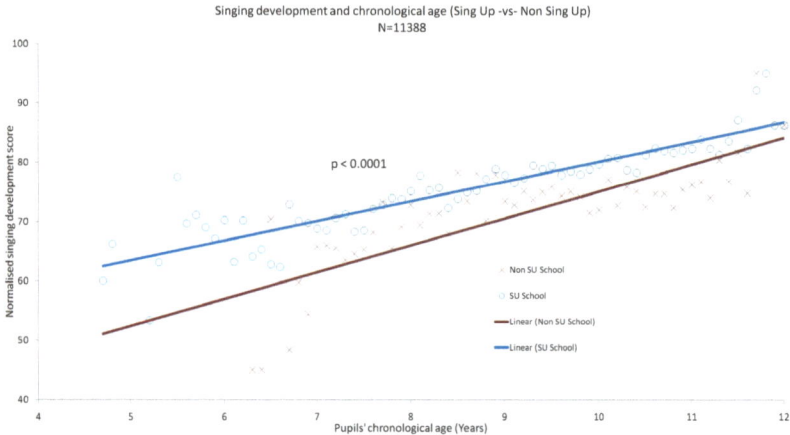

Figure 10: Singing development and chronological age

3.6 Children's singing development and age: impact of *Sing Up*

When children's normalised singing development scores were plotted against their chronological age, a clear difference emerges in the ratings between children who have experience of *Sing Up* and those who have not (figure 10). *Sing Up* experienced children tend to be approximately two years in advance of their non-*Sing Up* peers. Assessed differences range from approximately three years for the youngest children to one year for the oldest.

When the *Sing Up* data are broken down into their various composite school types (*Sing Up Award schools — Gold/Silver/Platinum*; *Chorister Outreach Programme* [COP]; *Workforce Development*; *Singing Playgrounds*) and compared with children's data from non-*Sing Up* schools, the developmental differences in children's singing are still evident (Figure 11) ($\mathscr{F}(7590, 286) = 4.317$, $p<.0001$). Each strand has children that, on average, are in advance developmentally of their non-*Sing Up* peers. Two of the three *Sing Up* interventions that embrace either a sustained focus on singing (as in the *Award schools*), or an intensive programme (under the *COP* umbrella) demonstrate the largest developmental differences. For the other two *Sing Up* interventions (termed

3 MAIN FINDINGS

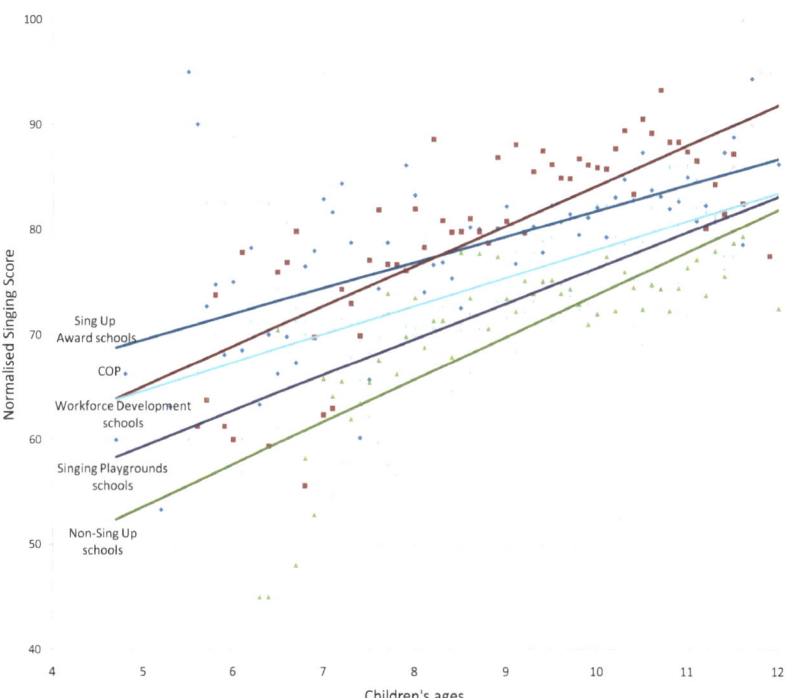

Figure 11: Singing development and chronological age by school type

3.7 Longitudinal evidence of *Sing Up*'s impact

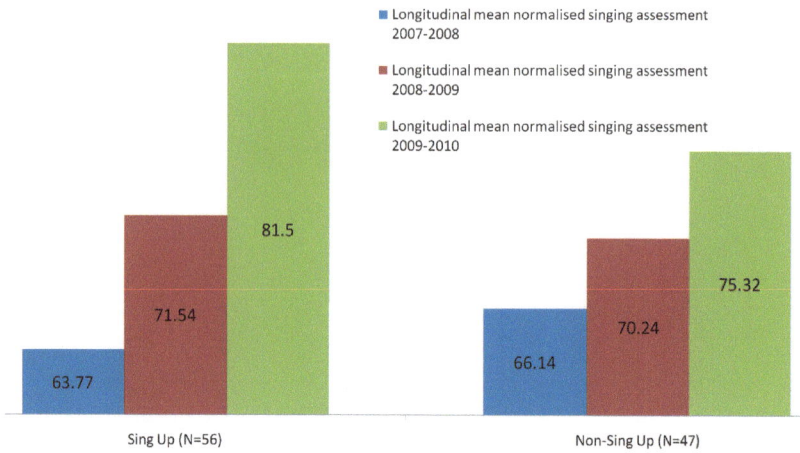

Figure 12: Longitudinal data and school type across three years

Workforce Development schools and *Singing Playgrounds Schools*[4]) the impact is less dramatic, but still evident.

3.7 Longitudinal evidence of *Sing Up*'s impact

Within the overall dataset, n=103 children have been assessed three times longitudinally. As might be expected from the overall data reported in figure 8, children tend to become more competent singers with age. However, the longitudinal data available across three years indicate that *Sing Up* experienced children develop significantly more ($p<.001$) compared to their non-*Sing Up* peers (see figure 12).

This trend is echoed in the longitudinal data analyses for children who were assessed twice, i.e., across two different school years, n=900 (see figure 13, $p<.001$).

In both instances (related to figures 12 and 13), there are no sex

---

[4]Much of the *Singing Playgrounds* data were collected in the first year (2007-2008) and this was early in the *Sing Up* programme. However, our latest data from the third year (2009-2010) indicates that the *Singing Playgrounds* developmental ratings are very much in line with those for the *Award schools* and *COP* and consistently higher than for non-*Sing Up* schools across all ages.

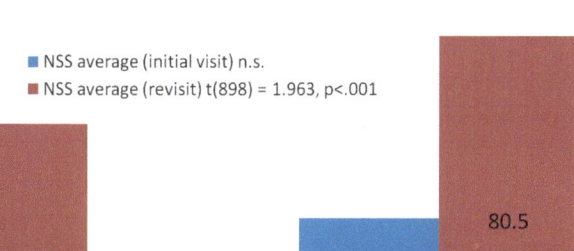

Figure 13: Longitudinal data and school type across two consecutive years (NSS = Normalised Singing Score — out of 100)

	% schools	
	Non *Sing Up*	*Sing Up*
upper quartile	13	87
lower quartile	43	57

Table 2: Proportions of *Sing Up* and non-*Sing Up* schools in an overall schools' ranking by upper and lower quartiles

differences evidenced in the changes in longitudinal data. Both sexes improved their singing over time.

3.8 Singing assessment and school type rankings

Sing Up Primary schools tend to cluster more towards the top of the overall ranking of schools currently on the database (n=177). In contrast, non-*Sing Up* schools, including those termed non-choristers in Cathedral schools, tend to be distributed more towards the bottom quartile (see table 2) ($\mathcal{X}^2$= 18.52, p<.001).

3.9 Attitudinal evidence and *Sing Up* impact

Analyses of the children's questionnaire responses (n=10,425) revealed that: Girls were more positive than boys on all six themes[5] ($p=.001$); Younger children tended to be more positive than older children*; and *Sing Up* experienced children tended to be more positive than non-*Sing Up* children about singing in school ($p=.001$).

3.10 Singing development, self concept and social inclusion

Within the singing focused statements (n=45) that embraced five themes (see footnote 4) were interspersed other statements (n=12 in 2008-09; n=15 in 2009-10[6]) that related to children's self-concept and sense of social inclusion.

When the children's (n=6639) answers to these questions were plotted against the same children's singing development ratings, a clear trend emerges. There is a positive linear relationship evidenced between children's singing development and their self-concept and sense of social inclusion. This is not to say that one 'causes' the other, but that the two aspects appear to be closely correlated (see figure 14).

Nevertheless, overall, separate questionnaire analyses reveal that *Sing Up* experienced children are more positive ($p<.05$) than their non-*Sing Up* peers about themselves and their sense of being part of community. And this positivity can be seen alongside the other trend evidenced earlier (figure 8) for *Sing Up* experienced children to be more advanced in their singing development. A clear inference may be drawn that children with experience of *Sing Up* are more likely to be advanced in their singing development and to have a positive self-concept.

---

[5]The six themes are:
1. Identity as a singer (emotional connection with singing)
2. Identity as a singer (self-efficacy)
3. Singing at home
4. Singing at school
5. Singing in informal settings
6. Self concept and sense of social inclusion

[6]Three questions were added from Achenbach (1991/2001) Child Behaviour Checklist to the original twelve from the Fitts (1964/1991) Tennessee Self Concept scale questionnaire.

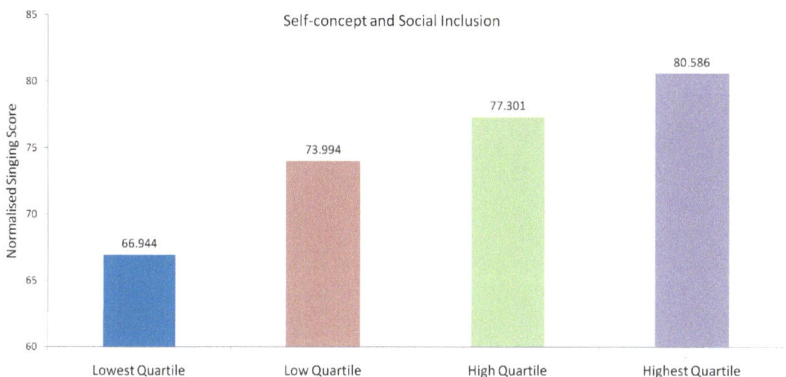

Figure 14: Self-concept and social inclusion means by quartile and normalised singing score for the same children (n=6639 children, 2008-2010)

4 Conclusions

Children's singing abilities and attitudes are socially and culturally located, subject to developmental processes and sensitive to educational experiences. Across the first three years of the research-based *Sing Up* impact evaluation, data have been collected from 9,979 children, involving 11,388 individual singing assessments and the completion of 10,245 singing and self focused attitudinal questionnaires.

Analyses of the data provide evidence that those children who have participated in the *Sing Up* programme are approximately two years in advance developmentally in their singing compared to their peers of the same age outside the programme.

In addition, *Sing Up* experienced children have more positive attitudes to singing in school and appear to have a more positive self-image as a result of these experiences.

5 References

Achenbach, T. M. (1991/2001). *Manual for Child Behavior Checklist 4-18, 1991 Profile.* Burlington, VT: University of Vermont, Department of Psychiatry.

Fitts, W.H. (1964). *The Fitts Tennessee Self Concept scale questionnaire.* Los Angeles: Western Psychological Services. (Updated Fitts, W.H., & Warren, W.L. (1991). Tennessee Self-Concept Scale: Second Edition (TSCS:2))

Rutkowski, J. (1997). The nature of children's singing voices: Characteristics and assessment. In: B.A. Roberts (Ed.), *The Phenomenon of Singing* (pp. 201-209). St. John's, NF: Memorial University Press.

Welch, G. F. (1998). Early childhood musical development. *Research Studies in Music Education, 11,* 27-41.

Welch, G.F., Himonides, E., Papageorgi, I., Saunders, J., Rinta, T., Stewart, C., Preti, C., Lani, J., Vraka, M. & Hill, J. (2009). The National Singing Programme for Primary schools in England: an initial baseline study. *Music Education Research, 11* (1). 1-22.

6 Selected Public Output related to *Sing Up*

Welch, G.F. (2008). The power of music in children's development. Invited keynote. *'Seminario: Apprendimento practico della musica e competenze trasversali'* , Bologna, 27 May.

Welch, G.F. (2008). The Psychology of Singing Development. Canterbury Christ Church University. *'The Phenomenon of Singing'* Seminar series, Invited speaker, Folkestone, UK, 3 June

Welch, G.F., Himonides, E., Saunders, J., Papageorgi, I., Rinta, T., Stewart, C., Preti, I. & Lani, J. (2008). The National Singing Programme for Primary schools In England: An Initial baseline study. *28th International Society for Music Education World Conference*, Invited speaker, Bologna, Italy, 20-25 July.

Welch, G.F., Saunders, J., Papageorgi, I., Himonides, E., Rinta, T., Preti, C., Stewart, C., Vraka, M. & Lani, J. (2008). An Assessment of Children's Singing Development in Primary Schools In England. *ICMPC10*, Invited Speaker, Sapporo, Japan, 25-29 August.

Welch, G.F., Saunders, J., Papageorgi, I., & Himonides, E. (2008). A Baseline Study of Children's Attitudes to Singing in English Primary Schools. 2nd *European Conference on Developmental Psychology of Music*. Invited Speaker, Roehampton University, UK, 10-12 September.

Welch, G.F. (2010) [on behalf of the research team]. The impact of the National Singing Programme *'Sing Up'* in England. *ISME 29th World Conference*, Beijing, China. 5 August.

Welch, G.F., Himonides, E., Saunders, J., Papageorgi, I., Rinta, T., Vraka, M. & Stephens Himonides, C. (2010). Children's singing development, self-concept and social inclusion. *ICMPC11*, Seattle, USA, 25 August.

7 Articles in refereed international journals

Welch, G.F. (2009). Evidence of the development of vocal pitch matching ability in children. *Japanese Journal of Music Education Research, 39*(1), 38-47.

Welch, G.F., Himonides, E., Papageorgi, I., Saunders, J., Rinta, T., Stewart, C., Preti, C., Lani, J., Vraka, M. & Hill, J. (2009). The National Singing Programme for Primary schools in England: an initial baseline study. *Music Education Research, 11*(1). 1-22.

Welch, G.F., Himonides, E., Saunders, J., Papageorgi, I., Rinta, T., Preti, C., Stewart, C., Lani, J. & Hill, J. (in press). Researching the first year of the National Singing Programme in England: an initial impact evaluation. *Psychomusicology: Music Mind and Brain.* [Special Issue on the Psychology of Singing] *21*(1).

Welch, G.F., Himonides, E., Saunders, J., Papageorgi, I., Vraka, M., Preti, C. & Stephens, C. (under review). Children's singing behaviour, development, attitudes to singing, self-concept and sense of social inclusion in the context of an impact evaluation of the National Singing Programme in England '*Sing Up*'. *Psychology of Music.*

8 Conference Proceedings

Welch, G.F., Himonides, E., Saunders, J., Papageorgi, I., Rinta, T., Stewart, C., Preti, C. & Lani, J. (2008). The National Singing Programme for Primary schools in England: An Initial Baseline Study. In W. Sims (Ed.). *Proceedings, International Society for Music Education 28th World Conference*, Bologna, Italy, 20-25 July, 2008, pp. 311-316.

Welch, G.F. (2009). Neuropsychobiological features of musical behaviour and development *[Original title: Νευροψυχοβιολογικά χαρακτηριστικά της μουσικής συμπεριφοράς και ανάπτυξης, Trans. E. Himonides]. Proceedings, 6th International Conference of the Greek Society of Music Education*, Athens 30 Oct-1 Nov. (www.eeme.gr) ISBN: 978-960-89847-5-2; English version pages: 24-37; Greek version pages: 356-371.

Welch, G.F., Himonides, E., Saunders, J., Papageorgi, I., Vraka, M. & Preti, C. (2009). Singing behaviour and development in English Primary schools: An impact analysis — evidence from the 2nd year of the National Singing Programme in England. In M. Argyriou, & P. Kampylis (Eds.), *Teaching Material and its contribution to educational practice: from theory to application in Music Education.* Proceedings of the 3rd GAPMET International Conference, Athens, Greece 8-10 May. (pp9-15). Athens: GAPMET [ISBN 987-960-89479-6-2].

9 Published reports

Welch, G.F., Himonides, E., Saunders, J., Papageorgi, I., Rinta, T., Preti, C., Stewart, C., Lani, J., Vraka, M. & Hill, J. (2008). *Researching the first year of the National Singing Programme in England: An initial impact evaluation of children's singing behaviours and singer identity.* London: Institute of Education. [pp 44] [[ISBN: 978-1-905351-09-1].

Welch, G.F., Himonides, E., Saunders, J., Papageorgi, I., Vraka, M., Preti, C. & Stephens, C. (2009). *Researching the second year of the National Singing Programme in England: An ongoing impact evaluation of children's singing behaviour and identity.* Institute of Education, University of London. [pp95]. [ISBN 978-1-905351-10-7].

Welch, G.F., Papageorgi, I., Vraka, M., Himonides, E. & Saunders, J. (2009). *The Chorister Outreach Programme: A Research Evaluation 2008-2009.* London: Institute of Education. [pp 52].

Saunders, J., Himonides, E. & Welch, G.F. (2010). Engaging with the National Singing Programme: *Sing Up* Live Field Study. London: Institute of Education. [pp69].

10 Other output in professional journals

Welch, G.F. (2008). *The benefits of Singing.* Sing Up Magazine, Spring 2008, http://tinyurl.com/2vv6mld

Welch, G.F. (2010). *Yes, we can!* Sing Up Magazine, Spring 2010, http://tinyurl.com/35ws6c8

www.ingramcontent.com/pod-product-compliance
Lightning Source LLC
Chambersburg PA
CBHW040059200426
43193CB00051B/17